Fact Finders®

PEOPLE YOU
SHOULD KNOW

JOHN McCAIN

Get to Know the Brave POW and Senator

by Dani Gabriel

Consultant: Christina Cliff
Assistant Professor of Political Science, Security Studies
Franklin Pierce University

CAPSTONE PRESS
a capstone imprint

Fact Finders Books are published by Capstone Press
1710 Roe Crest Drive, North Mankato, Minnesota 56003
www.capstonepub.com

Library of Congress Cataloging-in-Publication data is available on the Library of Congress website.
Names: Gabriel, Dani, author.
Title: John McCain : get to know the brave POW and Senator / by Dani Gabriel.
Description: First edition. | North Mankato, Minnesota : Capstone Press,
 [2020] | Series: Fact finders. People you should know | Includes
 bibliographical references and index. | Audience: Grades K–3. | Audience:
 Ages 8–9.
Identifiers: LCCN 2019005994 | ISBN 9781543571844 (hardcover) | ISBN
 9781543574661 (paperback) | ISBN 9781543571912 (ebook pdf)
Subjects: LCSH: McCain, John, 1936–2018—Juvenile literature. |
 Legislators—United States—Biography—Juvenile literature. | United
 States. Congress. Senate—Biography—Juvenile literature. | Prisoners of
 war—Vietnam—Biography—Juvenile literature. | Presidential
 candidates—United States—Biography.
Classification: LCC E840.8.M26 G33 2019 | DDC 328.73/092 [B]—dc23
LC record available at https://lccn.loc.gov/2019005994

Editorial Credits
Mari Bolte, editor; Kayla Rossow, designer; Tracy Cummins, media researcher; Tori Abraham, production specialist

Photo Credits
Alamy: Everett Collection Historical, 16, 17, Hum Historical, 18, 20; Getty Images: Cynthia Johnson/The LIFE Images Collection, 24, Denver Post, 23, Justin Sullivan, 29; Newscom: Darin Oswald/Idaho Statesman/MCT, Cover, Jack Kurtz/UPI Photo Service, 5, Keystone USA/ZUMA Press, 11, Lee K. Marriner/UPI Photo Service, 27, REUTERS/Jim Young, 6, REUTERS/SHANNON STAPLETON, 8; Shutterstock: Joseph Sohm, 13; Wikimedia: US Navy, 14

Source Notes
page 9, line 3: Associated Press. "McCain Counters Obama 'Arab' Question." https://www.youtube.com/watch?time_continue=67&v=jrnRU3ocIH4. Viewed March 23, 2019.

page 9, line 9: Ibid.

page 11, line 1: Claudia Grisales. "The McCains: A Military Legacy." https://www.stripes.com/news/special-reports/featured/mccain/the-mccains-a-military-legacy-1.532541. Viewed August 11, 2018.

page 13, line 8: Greg Daugherty. "John McCain in the Military: From Navy Brat to POW." https://www.history.com/news/john-mccain-navy-career-timeline-vietnam-pow. Viewed August 13, 2018.

page 19, line 6: John McCain. "John McCain, Prisoner of War: A First-Person Account." https://www.usnews.com/news/articles/2008/01/28/john-mccain-prisoner-of-war-a-first-person-account. Viewed August 13, 2018.

page 19, sidebar: Caroline Linton. "Revisiting Hanoi, Where John McCain Was Shot Down and Held as a POW." https://www.cbsnews.com/news/john-mccain-hanoi-hilton-prisoner-of-war-truc-bach-lake/. Viewed August 12, 2018.

page 20, line 10: Greg Daugherty.

page 22, line 7: Dan Nowicki and Bill Muller. "John McCain's Marriage, Move to Arizona Helped Launch Political Career." https://www.azcentral.com/story/news/politics/arizona/2018/04/02/john-mccain-move-arizona-marriage-cindy-mccain-helped-launch-political-career/538674001/. Viewed August 11, 2018.

page 26, line 13: "The 2000 Campaign; Excerpts from McCain's Speech." https://www.nytimes.com/2000/02/20/us/the-2000-campaign-excerpts-from-mccain-s-speech.html. Viewed August 12, 2018.

page 27, sidebar: "John McCain's Powerful Statement to the Khans." https://www.cnn.com/2016/08/01/politics/john-mccain-statement-khan-family/index.html. Viewed August 11, 2018.

All internet sites appearing in back matter were available and accurate when this book was sent to press.

Printed in the United States of America.
PA70

TABLE OF CONTENTS

THE CANDIDATE

Arizona Senator John McCain had a tough road ahead. He was running for president of the United States for the second time in his career. He had lost the Republican **nomination** in 2000. Now, in 2008, he wanted to win the nomination—and then the election.

Things had changed in eight years. During his first run for president, John had been a senator who had proven himself willing to fight against his party when he felt its members were wrong. He was a Vietnam War veteran with a hot temper, best known for speaking his mind. He was also an underdog to the other candidate in the Republican primary, George W. Bush. George was the son of George H.W. Bush, a former president.

While John's campaign started strong, he withdrew in March 2000 after losing a number of primary elections to George. His challenger went on to defeat the Democratic candidate, Al Gore, to become the president.

During his 2000 election run, John attracted Republican, Democratic, and independent voters with his promise of straight talk and change.

DID YOU KNOW?

Primary elections are held to decide which candidate from a political party will get to compete against candidates from other parties in elections. Voters can choose which candidates in their political party will be on the final voting **ballot**.

ballot—paper or mechanical method used to record a vote
nomination—the choice of someone as a candidate for political office

The 2008 election would be different. John had gained attention from his 2000 presidential run. Now John was a favorite among many voters who liked his direct, no-nonsense style.

More than 130 million people voted in the 2008 election, which was a record high until the 2016 election.

John liked to think of himself as a scrappy underdog. He was honest, and he never ran from a fight. But he wasn't afraid to give credit where credit was due. He often talked about his admiration for his opponents. He admitted when he thought he was wrong, and he worked hard to do better.

He also knew things couldn't get done if people didn't work together. As a representative and a senator, he was well known for his belief in **bipartisanship** and "working across the aisle." This meant he worked with Democratic politicians to reach compromises. As a speaker at the 2004 Republican National Convention, he said, "We are Americans first, Americans last, Americans always. Let us argue our differences. But remember we are not enemies."

By March 2008 John had won enough of the primary elections to guarantee his nomination to be the Republican presidential candidate. The race between Democratic candidates went on much longer. Senators Hillary Clinton and Barack Obama fought for their nominations until June, when Hillary **conceded**.

bipartisan—the cooperation between two political parties who usually oppose each other's policies

concede—to surrender or yield

The 2008 presidential election was the first time two sitting senators would run against each other.

Barack Obama would prove to be a tough opponent. One issue that John and Barack disagreed on was the Iraq War. The Iraq War had been going on for five years, and it was a hot-button issue among voters. Barack supported pulling troops out of the war zone. John wanted to win the war. He argued hard against many other opinions and policies supported by Barack. But he didn't let his personal and political issues get in the way of decency and respect for his opponent.

At a town hall meeting in Lakeville, Minnesota, an attendee remarked that she could not trust Barack because of his background. "He is a decent person and a person that you don't have to be scared of as president of the United States," John told her. The crowd booed him.

Another supporter took the microphone. She called Barack untrustworthy and "an Arab." John shook his head. "No, ma'am," he said, taking the mic away from her. "He's a decent family man and **citizen** that I just happen to have disagreements with . . . that's what the campaign's all about."

Throughout his career, John was known as many things—serviceman, pilot, war hero, senator, presidential nominee. But he was best known for being a "maverick," or someone who was not afraid to think or act independently.

DID YOU KNOW?

John's running mate for vice president was Alaska Governor Sarah Palin. It was the first time the Republican Party had nominated a woman for that role. Barack Obama's running mate was Delaware Senator Joe Biden. Both Barack and John were born outside the continental United States.

citizen—a member of a country or state who has the right to live there

2 > THE MCCAIN REPUTATION

John Sidney McCain III was born on August 29, 1936, at Coco Solo Naval Air Station in Panama. His mother, Roberta, called him "Johnny" his entire life. He had an older sister named Sandy and a younger brother named Joe.

The McCain family was a proud military family. John's first memory was of his father driving away to fight in World War II (1939–1945) when John was 5 years old. Both John's father, John Sidney "Jack" Jr., and grandfather, John Sidney "Slew," were naval officers. They were the first father and son to reach the rank of four-star admiral, generally considered the highest rank for a Navy officer. In the early 1990s a Naval destroyer was named for them.

John with his father and grandfather. In 2018 the U.S. Navy added John's name to the USS *John S. McCain.*

"For two centuries, the men of my family were raised to go to war as officers in America's armed services," John wrote later. "When my own time at war arrived, I realized how fortunate I was to have been raised in such a family."

As a military family, the McCains moved around a lot. They lived on naval bases all over the world. John attended 20 different schools by the time he graduated high school. His last three years of school were spent at Episcopal High School, a private boarding school, in Alexandria, Virginia.

John was on the smaller side but was known among his classmates for his fiery temper. He was a star wrestler, earning his high school letter in his first year. He also played football and tennis, belonged to the campus literary society, and worked on the school newspaper and the yearbook.

After graduation, John followed the family tradition of service and enrolled at the U.S. Naval Academy in 1954. Both his father and grandfather had attended the Annapolis, Maryland, school. Although John sometimes bragged about his notable ancestry, he graduated fifth from the bottom of his class.

By the time he graduated, John had already been accepted for flight school in Florida, and later Texas, to train as a pilot. He had a reputation of being fearless both in the sky and on the ground. In 1960 he was involved in a plane crash. The official Navy report said the accident was due to "operator error." He had additional mishaps in 1961 and 1965. "John was what you called a push-the-envelope guy," a fellow pilot said later.

In 1965 John married Carol Shepp. They had met when John was at the Naval Academy, and reconnected in 1964. She already had two children, Doug and Andy. A third child, Sidney, was born in 1966.

John's reputation for rule-breaking fun at the academy landed him with the nickname "John Wayne McCain," after Hollywood tough-guy John Wayne.

OFF TO WAR

John was **deployed** at the end of 1966 and went to Vietnam in June 1967. He served aboard the USS *Forrestal*. At the end of July, John was injured on board the aircraft carrier. He was waiting his turn to take off when another plane accidentally fired a missile.

The missile struck a plane near John, causing a fire. The flames moved throughout the carrier, causing bombs loaded onto planes to explode. John managed to escape his own plane, but **shrapnel** from the exploding bombs caught him in the chest and legs. He was also burned.

In all, 134 sailors were killed and another 161 were injured during the fire on the *Forrestal*. It was the worst loss of life on a Navy ship since World War II (1939–1945).

The Vietnam War

The Vietnam War (1959–1975) was fought primarily to prevent a North Vietnamese communist takeover of South Vietnam. North Vietnam, led by Ho Chi Minh, was supported by the communist Soviet Union and China. The United States, which was anti-communist, sided with South Vietnam. The conflict would expand into Laos and Cambodia as well. By the time John deployed, there were nearly 500,000 active U.S. troops in Vietnam.

The United States and North Vietnam ended their fighting in 1973 when the U.S. pulled out the last of its troops. But the war between North Vietnam and South Vietnam continued for two more years until North Vietnam eventually took over South Vietnam. About 2 million people, including 58,220 Americans, were killed. Another 2 million Vietnamese were wounded and 1.6 million became war **refugees**.

deploy—to move troops or equipment into position for military action

refugee—a person forced to flee his or her home because of natural disaster, war, or persecution

shrapnel—pieces that have broken off from an explosive shell

John flew an A-4 Skyhawk, a fast, lightweight bomber. His unit took part in some of the most dangerous missions. One-third of the pilots in his unit were either killed or captured that year.

In October 1967, John was on his 23rd bombing run over North Vietnam, a mission to destroy a **thermal power plant** in Hanoi, Vietnam. A missile destroyed the wing of John's plane, and he ejected at high speed. He broke his right leg and both of his arms. He landed in the middle of a lake. After managing to inflate his life vest, he fainted. He woke up to people dragging him out of the lake. He was beaten before being taken as a prisoner of war.

John (front, right) with his squadron in 1967.

A photo of John (center) being captured was sent from Vietnam to Tokyo. Reports of his capture were described over the radio.

The Hanoi Hilton

The Hoa Lò prison was in the middle of Hanoi, the capital city of North Vietnam. Prisoners of war sarcastically called it the "Hanoi Hilton." It was originally used by French colonists for their political prisoners. The prisoners were often tortured or executed. Starvation, filthy conditions, chains, and **solitary confinement** were part of everyday life at the Hanoi Hilton.

solitary confinement—keeping a prisoner in a separate cell as punishment
thermal power plant—a power plant that converts heat to electric power

John needed medical care. But his captors wanted information. John gave them his name, rank, and identification number, but nothing else. He spent the next four days in pain, drifting in and out of consciousness.

Eventually the guards found out that their prisoner's father was a **decorated** admiral. They called John the "Crown Prince." They offered to let him go early. But John knew that prisoners of war were exchanged in the order they had been captured. He knew he was not next in line, and so he refused their offer. In 1968 he was put in solitary confinement. He was alone for the next two years.

The Hanoi Hilton was only one of many prisoner-of-war camps around the city. No one ever escaped the Hanoi Hilton.

During his time in prison, John was forced to make recordings that were later used for **propaganda**. He also signed a false confession that said he was a war criminal. In both instances, John suffered beatings and torture for days before giving in. As John later described it, "I had learned what we all learned over there: Every man has his breaking point. I had reached mine."

He was finally released in 1973. After five and a half years as a prisoner, he was **malnourished**. His broken bones had not healed correctly. Although he was only 36 years old, his hair was white. It took him months to recover. He was never able to raise his arms above his head again.

After the War

"There is no reason for me to hold a grudge or anger. There's certainly some individual guards who were very cruel and inflicted a lot of pain on me and others but there's certainly no sense in me hating the Vietnamese. . . . I hold no ill will toward them." —John McCain

decorated—awarded medals
malnourish—to inadequately feed someone
propaganda—information spread to try to influence the thinking of people

John met President Richard Nixon at the White House in May 1973. The men continued to write to each other until Richard's death in 1994. The Nixon family attended John's funeral in 2018.

John was welcomed home in Jacksonville, Florida. The city threw a parade to celebrate the returning war hero. The mayor gave him the key to the city. He visited the White House. He used his time after the war to speak to people. John traveled around the country, telling his story. He also spent months doing physical therapy to try to recover from his injuries.

During his rehabilitation, John attended the National War College in Washington, D.C. "By the time my nine months at the War College ended, I had satisfied my curiosity about how Americans had entered and lost the Vietnam War," he said.

In 1977 he was able to pass a physical exam in order to fly again. He started training pilots at Cecil Field in Jacksonville. He also began working in the Senate **liaison** office in Washington, D.C. He represented the Navy and worked to get support in Congress for naval projects. While in this position, he met Cindy Hensley. In February 1980 John divorced Carol. Their relationship had suffered after he returned from the war. Shortly after, he and Cindy married and moved to Arizona. They would have three children together and adopt a fourth from Bangladesh.

Honors

In 1981 John realized he wasn't likely to be promoted again because of his injuries. He retired from the Navy as a captain. Some of the honors he received were the Silver Star, two Legion of Merits, three Bronze Stars, two Purple Hearts, and the Prisoner of War Medal.

liaison—someone who establishes contact and understanding between two groups

4 ❯ A LIFE IN POLITICS

His time in the Senate liaison office had given John a taste for politics. In 1982 he ran for the House of Representatives.

Because the McCains had just recently moved to Arizona, many critics called John a **carpetbagger**. Finally, John had had enough. "Listen pal," he said, addressing his opponent, "I spent 22 years in the Navy. We in the military service tend to move around a lot. We have to live in all parts of the country, all parts of the world. I wish I could have had the luxury, like you, of . . . spending my entire life in a nice place like the first district of Arizona, but I was doing other things. As a matter of fact, when I think about it now, the place I lived longest in my life was Hanoi."

The audience was speechless. John won the election with more than twice the number of votes as his opponent.

carpetbagger—a political candidate who runs for election in an area where he or she has no local connections

John was a popular House member. He was elected the president of the Republican freshman class of representatives in 1983. This meant he would lead and represent the other incoming politicians in their first year.

Grab Your Bags

After the Civil War (1861–1865), the Southern states were in bad shape. Rebuilding those places was called Reconstruction. Northerners who moved to the South during this time were called carpetbaggers. It was thought that they had come to take advantage of the situation to get rich or to grab political power. The name came from the idea that they could carry everything they owned in a carpetbag.

John served two terms as the Arizona representative. But that wasn't enough for him. In early 1985 he announced he would run for a Senate seat. On election day in 1986, he won 60 percent of the vote. He would serve the state of Arizona as a senator until his death in 2018.

John really made a name for himself in the Senate. He was particularly concerned with the military. He was a member, and later the chairman, of the Senate Armed Services Committee. Now, instead of **lobbying** for military interests, he was making decisions on them.

John, Cindy, and two of their children with President George H.W. Bush in 1987 at the Senate swearing-in.

John was also concerned about veterans. He was one of the co-sponsors of the Americans with Disabilities Act in 1990. The ADA protects disabled people from **discrimination**. It also gives them equal access to public facilities, transportation, employment, and other services.

In 2005 John worked with Democratic Senator Dianne Feinstein of California to pass the Detainee Treatment Act. The act banned the military from using torture and allowed the Red Cross to have access to prisoners of war.

Senate Committees

The Senate has 20 permanent committees. The main job of the committees is to discuss bills that may be signed into law. They research the issues relating to the bill, make changes, and then vote on whether or not to approve the bill. The Senate committees John served on were Armed Services, Foreign Relations, Indian Affairs, Homeland Security and Government Affairs, and the Senate Select Committee on POW/MIA Affairs.

discrimination—unfair treatment of a person or group
lobby—to try to persuade government officials to act or vote in a certain way

AIMING HIGH

In 2000 John ran for the Republican presidential nomination. Texas Governor George W. Bush was the party's favored candidate. He had more money and more supporters. In response, John launched a bus tour he called the "Straight Talk Express." He held town halls across the country. His growing popularity surprised a lot of people.

But in the end, he lost the nomination. Some felt that John didn't respond well to negative press coverage of his campaign. "I will not take the low road to the highest office in this land," John said after his defeat. "I want the presidency in the best way, not the worst way." He returned to the Senate and got back to work.

DID YOU KNOW?

Politicians often hold small gatherings called town halls. At these events, constituents can ask their elected officials questions and let them know their opinions. John was great at hosting these events. He spoke directly and honestly about his views. This got him a lot of attention.

The Straight Talk Express traveled all over the country. One driver alone logged 70,000 miles (112,654 kilometers) behind the wheel.

In 2003 the United States invaded Iraq, with the goal of overthrowing the country's leader, Saddam Hussein. The invasion led to the Iraq War (2003–2011). People around the world held protests. John was criticized often for his ongoing support of the war. He firmly believed that the United States should send even more troops into the war zone.

Standing Up for Heroes

Army Captain Humayun Khan was killed in Iraq in 2004. In 2016 his parents, Khizr and Ghazala Khan, attended the Democratic National Convention. During the convention, Khizr condemned Republican nominee Donald Trump's criticisms of immigrants and, particularly, Muslim immigrants. In turn, Trump attacked Khizr's family. John did not stand by quietly.

"I'd like to say to Mr. and Mrs. Khan: Thank you for immigrating to America. We're a better country because of you. And you are certainly right; your son was the best of America, and the memory of his sacrifice will make us a better nation—and he will never be forgotten," John said.

Although John's campaign for the 2008 presidential election was not successful, he continued his life in politics. And he continued to be a maverick. He acted on his ideals, even if they didn't agree with his party's line.

The Affordable Care Act (ACA) was signed into law on March 23, 2010. The act, also known as Obamacare, gave millions of Americans access to health care. Many Republicans, John included, did not initially support the ACA. They believed the government should not be involved in requiring health insurance. John even made repealing the ACA part of his Senate re-election campaigns in 2010 and 2016. He continued to work to replace the ACA.

In 2017 John was diagnosed with glioblastoma, an advanced kind of brain cancer. But he kept working. And he showed up for an important vote. On July 28, 2017, the Republican-controlled Congress was voting on a bill that would **repeal** the ACA. There were 49 votes for the repeal, and 50 against. If the votes tied, Vice President Mike Pence would be the tiebreaker, and everyone knew he would vote to repeal.

John didn't think the process to repeal the ACA had been fair. He had always hated bullies. He had not been expected to show up to vote. But he did. He walked onto the Senate floor. He gave a thumbs-down, voting against the bill to repeal the ACA. Then he returned to his seat.

John leaving the Senate chamber after voting against the ACA repeal in 2017.

John's vote on the ACA was his last big stand in Congress. On August 25, 2018, John passed away. Before his death, he asked former President Barack Obama to speak at his funeral. He wanted to show the country that rivals can respect one another and work together. This was his greatest legacy.

repeal—to officially cancel something, such as a law

GLOSSARY

ballot (BAL-uht)—paper or mechanical methods used to record a vote

bipartisan (bye-PAR-tuh-suhn)—the cooperation between two political parties who usually oppose each other's policies

carpetbagger (KAR-puht BAY-guhr)—a political candidate who runs for election in an area where he or she has no local connections

citizen (SI-tuh-zuhn)—a member of a country or state who has the right to live there

communist (KAHM-yuh-nist)—country or person practicing communism; communism is a political system in which there is no private property and everything is owned by the government

concede (kahn-SEED)—to surrender or yield

decorated (DECK-o-ray-tid)—awarded medals

deploy (di-PLOY)—to move troops or equipment into position for military action

discrimination (dis-kri-muh-NAY-shuhn)—unfair treatment of a person or group, often because of race, religion, gender, sexual preference, or age

liaison (lee-AY-zuhn)—someone who establishes contact and understanding between two groups

lobby (LOB-ee)—to try to persuade government officials to act or vote in a certain way

malnourish (mal-NUR-ish)—to inadequately feed someone

nomination (NOM-uh-nay-shuhn)—choosing someone as a candidate for political office

propaganda (prop-ah-GAN-da)—information spread to try to influence the thinking of people; often not completely true or fair

refugee (ref-yuh-JEE)—a person forced to flee his or her home because of natural disaster, war, or persecution

repeal (ri-PEEL)—to officially cancel something, such as a law

shrapnel (SHRAP-huhl)—pieces that have broken off from an explosive shell

solitary confinement (SOL-uh-ter-ee kuhn-FINE-mehnt)—keeping a prisoner in a separate cell as punishment

thermal power plant (THUR-muhl POW-ur PLANT)—a power plant that converts heat to electric power

READ MORE

Gormley, Beatrice. *John McCain: An American Hero*. New York: Aladdin/Simon & Schuster, 2018.

MacCarald, Clara. *Living Through the Vientam War*. Vero Beach, FL: Rourke Educational Media, 2019.

Schwartz, Heather E. *John McCain: The Courage of Conviction*. Minneapolis: Lerner Publications, 2019.

WEBSITES

Britannic Kids: Vietnam War
https://kids.britannica.com/students/article/Vietnam-War/277599

John McCain
https://www.johnmccain.com/

United States Senate
https://www.senate.gov/

CRITICAL THINKING QUESTIONS

1. John was known as someone who spoke his mind. Go back and re-read some of John's quotes. Do you agree with any of them? Why or why not?

2. John's time in Vietnam was one of the most difficult parts of his life. Imagine what it would have been like to be a prisoner for five years. How do you think it changed the way John lived his life?

3. Coming from a military family, John often felt pressure to succeed in the armed forces too. Identify a situation where he tried to stand out from or be independent of his family's reputation.

INDEX